This Feelings Journal Belongs To:

_____

My Feelings Journal © 2019 by Matilda Boyd

All rights reserved. No part of this book may be used or reproduced in any manner whatsoever without written permission except in the case of brief quotations embodied in critical articles and reviews.
First edition: 2019

Date: _____

Today I feel _____.

😊 😍 😜 😟 😢 😬 😠

This is a picture of how I'm feeling today ...

I feel this way because ...

_____
_____
_____
_____
_____
_____
_____

Something that might help me feel better is ...

_____
_____
_____
_____
_____

Picture of me doing this ...

Someone who I would like to share my feelings with is _____.

I will do this by talking to them / writing them a note. (Circle one)

Dear _____,

Today I feel _____

because _____

_____

_____

_____

_____

_____

_____

_____

_____

_____

_____

_____

_____

*The back of this page is left blank so that you can draw a picture of how you feel and tear this page out of your journal to give someone your message.

Date: _____

Today I feel _____.

This is a picture of how I'm feeling today ...

I feel this way because ...

_____
_____
_____
_____
_____
_____
_____

Something that might help me feel better is ...

_____

_____

_____

_____

_____

Picture of me doing this ...

Someone who I would like to share my feelings with is _____.

I will do this by talking to them / writing them a note. (Circle one)

Dear _____,

Today I feel _____

because _____

_____

_____

_____

_____

_____

_____

_____

_____

_____

_____

_____

_____

_____

*The back of this page is left blank so that you can draw a picture of how you feel and tear this page out of your journal to give someone your message.

Date: _____

Today I feel _____.

😊 😍 🤪 😟 😢 😬 😠

This is a picture of how I'm feeling today ...

I feel this way because ...

_____
_____
_____
_____
_____
_____
_____

Something that might help me feel better is ...

_____
_____
_____
_____
_____

Picture of me doing this ...

Someone who I would like to share my feelings with is _____.

I will do this by talking to them / writing them a note. (Circle one)

Dear _____,

Today I feel _____

because _____

_____

_____

_____

_____

_____

_____

_____

_____

_____

_____

_____

_____

_____

*The back of this page is left blank so that you can draw a picture of how you feel and tear this page out of your journal to give someone your message.

Date: _____

Today I feel _____.

😀 😍 🤪 😟 😢 😬 😠

This is a picture of how I'm feeling today ...

I feel this way because ...

_____
_____
_____
_____
_____
_____
_____

Something that might help me feel better is ...

_____

_____

_____

_____

_____

_____

Picture of me doing this ...

Someone who I would like to share my feelings with is _____.

I will do this by talking to them / writing them a note. (Circle one)

Dear _____,

Today I feel _____

because _____

_____

_____

_____

_____

_____

_____

_____

_____

_____

_____

_____

*The back of this page is left blank so that you can draw a picture of how you feel and tear this page out of your journal to give someone your message.

Date: _____

Today I feel _____.

This is a picture of how I'm feeling today ...

I feel this way because ...

_____
_____
_____
_____
_____
_____
_____

Something that might help me feel better is ...

_____

_____

_____

_____

_____

Picture of me doing this ...

Someone who I would like to share my feelings with is _____.

I will do this by talking to them / writing them a note. (Circle one)

Dear _____,

Today I feel _____

because _____

_____

_____

_____

_____

_____

_____

_____

_____

_____

_____

_____

_____

_____

*The back of this page is left blank so that you can draw a picture of how you feel and tear this page out of your journal to give someone your message.

Date: _____

Today I feel _____.

This is a picture of how I'm feeling today ...

I feel this way because ...

_____
_____
_____
_____
_____
_____
_____

Something that might help me feel better is ...

_____

_____

_____

_____

_____

_____

Picture of me doing this ...

Someone who I would like to share my feelings with is _____.

I will do this by talking to them / writing them a note. (Circle one)

Dear _____,

Today I feel _____

because _____

_____

_____

_____

_____

_____

_____

_____

_____

_____

_____

_____

_____

*The back of this page is left blank so that you can draw a picture of how you feel and tear this page out of your journal to give someone your message.

Date: _____

Today I feel _____.

😊 😍 😜 😟 😢 😁 😠

This is a picture of how I'm feeling today ...

I feel this way because ...

_____
_____
_____
_____
_____
_____
_____

Something that might help me feel better is ...

_____
_____
_____
_____
_____
_____

Picture of me doing this ...

Someone who I would like to share my feelings with is _____.

I will do this by talking to them / writing them a note. (Circle one)

Dear _____,

Today I feel _____

because _____

_____

_____

_____

_____

_____

_____

_____

_____

_____

_____

_____

_____

_____

*The back of this page is left blank so that you can draw a picture of how you feel and tear this page out of your journal to give someone your message.

Date: _____

Today I feel _____.

😀 😍 😜 😟 😢 😁 😠

This is a picture of how I'm feeling today ...

I feel this way because ...

_____
_____
_____
_____
_____
_____
_____
_____

Something that might help me feel better is ...

_____
_____
_____
_____
_____
_____

Picture of me doing this ...

Someone who I would like to share my feelings with is _____.

I will do this by talking to them / writing them a note. (Circle one)

Dear _____,

Today I feel _____

because _____

_____

_____

_____

_____

_____

_____

_____

_____

_____

_____

_____

*The back of this page is left blank so that you can draw a picture of how you feel and tear this page out of your journal to give someone your message.

Date: _____

Today I feel _____.

This is a picture of how I'm feeling today ...

I feel this way because ...

_____
_____
_____
_____
_____
_____
_____

Something that might help me feel better is ...

_____
_____
_____
_____
_____
_____

Picture of me doing this ...

Someone who I would like to share my feelings with is _____.

I will do this by talking to them / writing them a note. (Circle one)

Dear _____,

Today I feel _____

because _____

_____

_____

_____

_____

_____

_____

_____

_____

_____

_____

_____

_____

_____

_____

*The back of this page is left blank so that you can draw a picture of how you feel and tear this page out of your journal to give someone your message.

Date: _____

Today I feel _____.

😊 😍 😜 😟 😢 😬 😠

This is a picture of how I'm feeling today …

I feel this way because …

_____
_____
_____
_____
_____
_____
_____

Something that might help me feel better is ...

_____

_____

_____

_____

_____

Picture of me doing this ...

Someone who I would like to share my feelings with is _____.

I will do this by talking to them / writing them a note. (Circle one)

Dear _____,

Today I feel _____

because _____

_____

_____

_____

_____

_____

_____

_____

_____

_____

_____

_____

_____

*The back of this page is left blank so that you can draw a picture of how you feel and tear this page out of your journal to give someone your message.

Date: _____

Today I feel _____.

😊 😍 😜 😟 😢 😬 😠

This is a picture of how I'm feeling today ...

I feel this way because ...

_____
_____
_____
_____
_____
_____
_____

Something that might help me feel better is ...

_____
_____
_____
_____
_____
_____

Picture of me doing this ...

Someone who I would like to share my feelings with is _____.

I will do this by talking to them / writing them a note. (Circle one)

Dear _____,

Today I feel _____

because _____

_____

_____

_____

_____

_____

_____

_____

_____

_____

_____

*The back of this page is left blank so that you can draw a picture of how you feel and tear this page out of your journal to give someone your message.

Date: _____

Today I feel _____.

This is a picture of how I'm feeling today ...

I feel this way because ...

_____
_____
_____
_____
_____
_____
_____

Something that might help me feel better is ...

_____

_____

_____

_____

_____

Picture of me doing this ...

Someone who I would like to share my feelings with is _____.

I will do this by talking to them / writing them a note. (Circle one)

Dear _____,

Today I feel _____

because _____

_____

_____

_____

_____

_____

_____

_____

_____

_____

_____

_____

_____

_____

*The back of this page is left blank so that you can draw a picture of how you feel and tear this page out of your journal to give someone your message.

Date: _____

Today I feel _____.

This is a picture of how I'm feeling today ...

I feel this way because ...

_____
_____
_____
_____
_____
_____
_____

Something that might help me feel better is ...

_____
_____
_____
_____
_____

Picture of me doing this ...

Someone who I would like to share my feelings with is _____.

I will do this by talking to them / writing them a note. (Circle one)

Dear _____,

Today I feel _____

because _____

_____

_____

_____

_____

_____

_____

_____

_____

_____

_____

_____

_____

_____

*The back of this page is left blank so that you can draw a picture of how you feel and tear this page out of your journal to give someone your message.

Date: _____

Today I feel _____.

😊 😍 😜 😟 😢 😁 😠

This is a picture of how I'm feeling today ...

I feel this way because ...

_____
_____
_____
_____
_____
_____
_____

Something that might help me feel better is ...

_____
_____
_____
_____
_____

Picture of me doing this ...

Someone who I would like to share my feelings with is _____.

I will do this by talking to them / writing them a note. (Circle one)

Dear _____,

Today I feel _____

because _____

_____

_____

_____

_____

_____

_____

_____

_____

_____

_____

_____

_____

_____

*The back of this page is left blank so that you can draw a picture of how you feel and tear this page out of your journal to give someone your message.

Date: _____

Today I feel _____.

This is a picture of how I'm feeling today ...

I feel this way because ...

_____
_____
_____
_____
_____
_____
_____
_____

Something that might help me feel better is ...

_____
_____
_____
_____
_____

Picture of me doing this ...

Someone who I would like to share my feelings with is _____.

I will do this by talking to them / writing them a note. (Circle one)

Dear _____,

Today I feel _____

because _____

_____

_____

_____

_____

_____

_____

_____

_____

_____

_____

_____

_____

*The back of this page is left blank so that you can draw a picture of how you feel and tear this page out of your journal to give someone your message.

Date: _____

Today I feel _____.

😊 😍 😜 😟 😢 😁 😠

This is a picture of how I'm feeling today ...

I feel this way because ...

_____
_____
_____
_____
_____
_____
_____

Something that might help me feel better is ...

_____

_____

_____

_____

_____

Picture of me doing this ...

Someone who I would like to share my feelings with is _____.

I will do this by talking to them / writing them a note. (Circle one)

Dear _____,

Today I feel _____

because _____

_____

_____

_____

_____

_____

_____

_____

_____

_____

_____

_____

_____

*The back of this page is left blank so that you can draw a picture of how you feel and tear this page out of your journal to give someone your message.

Date: _____

Today I feel _____.

😊 😍 😜 😟 😢 😬 😠

This is a picture of how I'm feeling today ...

I feel this way because ...

_____
_____
_____
_____
_____
_____
_____

Something that might help me feel better is ...

_____

_____

_____

_____

_____

Picture of me doing this ...

Someone who I would like to share my feelings with is _____.

I will do this by talking to them / writing them a note. (Circle one)

Dear _____,

Today I feel _____

because _____

_____

_____

_____

_____

_____

_____

_____

_____

_____

_____

_____

_____

*The back of this page is left blank so that you can draw a picture of how you feel and tear this page out of your journal to give someone your message.

Date: _____

Today I feel _____.

😊 😍 😜 😟 😢 😬 😠

This is a picture of how I'm feeling today ...

I feel this way because ...

_____
_____
_____
_____
_____
_____
_____

Something that might help me feel better is ...

_____
_____
_____
_____
_____
_____

Picture of me doing this ...

Someone who I would like to share my feelings with is _____.

I will do this by talking to them / writing them a note. (Circle one)

Dear _____,

Today I feel _____

because _____

_____

_____

_____

_____

_____

_____

_____

_____

_____

_____

_____

_____

*The back of this page is left blank so that you can draw a picture of how you feel and tear this page out of your journal to give someone your message.

Date: _____

Today I feel _____.

😊 😍 😜 😟 😢 😬 😠

This is a picture of how I'm feeling today …

```
┌─────────────────────────────────────┐
│                                     │
│                                     │
│                                     │
│                                     │
│                                     │
└─────────────────────────────────────┘
```

I feel this way because …

_____

_____

_____

_____

_____

_____

_____

Something that might help me feel better is ...

_____
_____
_____
_____
_____
_____

Picture of me doing this ...

Someone who I would like to share my feelings with is _____.

I will do this by talking to them / writing them a note. (Circle one)

Dear _____,

Today I feel _____

because _____

_____

_____

_____

_____

_____

_____

_____

_____

_____

_____

_____

_____

_____

*The back of this page is left blank so that you can draw a picture of how you feel and tear this page out of your journal to give someone your message.

Date: _____

Today I feel _____.

This is a picture of how I'm feeling today ...

I feel this way because ...

_____
_____
_____
_____
_____
_____
_____

Something that might help me feel better is ...

_____
_____
_____
_____
_____
_____

Picture of me doing this ...

Someone who I would like to share my feelings with is _____.

I will do this by talking to them / writing them a note. (Circle one)

Dear _____,

Today I feel _____

because _____

_____

_____

_____

_____

_____

_____

_____

_____

_____

_____

_____

_____

_____

*The back of this page is left blank so that you can draw a picture of how you feel and tear this page out of your journal to give someone your message.

Date: _____

Today I feel _____.

😊 😍 😜 😟 😢 😁 😠

This is a picture of how I'm feeling today …

I feel this way because …

_____
_____
_____
_____
_____
_____
_____

Something that might help me feel better is ...

_____
_____
_____
_____
_____
_____

Picture of me doing this ...

Someone who I would like to share my feelings with is _____.

I will do this by talking to them / writing them a note. (Circle one)

Dear _____,

Today I feel _____

because _____

_____

_____

_____

_____

_____

_____

_____

_____

_____

_____

_____

_____

_____

*The back of this page is left blank so that you can draw a picture of how you feel and tear this page out of your journal to give someone your message.

Date: _____

Today I feel _____.

😀 😍 😜 😟 😢 😬 😠

This is a picture of how I'm feeling today ...

I feel this way because ...

_____
_____
_____
_____
_____
_____
_____

Something that might help me feel better is ...

_____
_____
_____
_____
_____
_____

Picture of me doing this ...

Someone who I would like to share my feelings with is _____.

I will do this by talking to them / writing them a note. (Circle one)

Dear _____,

Today I feel _____

because _____

_____
_____
_____
_____
_____
_____
_____
_____
_____
_____
_____
_____
_____
_____

*The back of this page is left blank so that you can draw a picture of how you feel and tear this page out of your journal to give someone your message.

Date: _____

Today I feel _____.

😊 😍 😜 😟 😢 😬 😠

This is a picture of how I'm feeling today ...

I feel this way because ...

_____
_____
_____
_____
_____
_____
_____
_____

Something that might help me feel better is ...

_____
_____
_____
_____
_____

Picture of me doing this ...

Someone who I would like to share my feelings with is _____.

I will do this by talking to them / writing them a note. (Circle one)

Dear _____,

Today I feel _____

because _____

_____

_____

_____

_____

_____

_____

_____

_____

_____

_____

_____

_____

*The back of this page is left blank so that you can draw a picture of how you feel and tear this page out of your journal to give someone your message.

Date: _____

Today I feel _____.

😊 😍 😜 😟 😢 😬 😠

This is a picture of how I'm feeling today ...

I feel this way because ...

_____
_____
_____
_____
_____
_____
_____

Something that might help me feel better is ...

_____
_____
_____
_____
_____
_____

Picture of me doing this ...

Someone who I would like to share my feelings with is _____.

I will do this by talking to them / writing them a note. (Circle one)

Dear _____,

Today I feel _____

because _____

_____

_____

_____

_____

_____

_____

_____

_____

_____

_____

_____

_____

_____

_____

*The back of this page is left blank so that you can draw a picture of how you feel and tear this page out of your journal to give someone your message.

Date: _____

Today I feel _____.

This is a picture of how I'm feeling today …

I feel this way because …

_____

_____

_____

_____

_____

_____

_____

Something that might help me feel better is ...

_____
_____
_____
_____
_____
_____

Picture of me doing this ...

Someone who I would like to share my feelings with is _____.

I will do this by talking to them / writing them a note. (Circle one)

Dear _____,

Today I feel _____

because _____

_____

_____

_____

_____

_____

_____

_____

_____

_____

_____

_____

_____

_____

_____

*The back of this page is left blank so that you can draw a picture of how you feel and tear this page out of your journal to give someone your message.

Date: _____

Today I feel _____.

😊 😍 😜 😟 😢 😁 😠

This is a picture of how I'm feeling today …

I feel this way because …

_____
_____
_____
_____
_____
_____
_____
_____

Something that might help me feel better is ...

_____
_____
_____
_____
_____
_____

Picture of me doing this ...

Someone who I would like to share my feelings with is _____.

I will do this by talking to them / writing them a note. (Circle one)

Dear _____,

Today I feel _____

because _____

_____

_____

_____

_____

_____

_____

_____

_____

_____

_____

_____

_____

*The back of this page is left blank so that you can draw a picture of how you feel and tear this page out of your journal to give someone your message.

Date: _____

Today I feel _____.

This is a picture of how I'm feeling today ...

I feel this way because ...

_____
_____
_____
_____
_____
_____
_____

Something that might help me feel better is ...

_____
_____
_____
_____
_____
_____

Picture of me doing this ...

Someone who I would like to share my feelings with is _____.

I will do this by talking to them / writing them a note. (Circle one)

Dear _____,

Today I feel _____

because _____

_____

_____

_____

_____

_____

_____

_____

_____

_____

_____

_____

_____

*The back of this page is left blank so that you can draw a picture of how you feel and tear this page out of your journal to give someone your message.

Date: _____

Today I feel _____.

This is a picture of how I'm feeling today ...

I feel this way because ...

_____
_____
_____
_____
_____
_____
_____

Something that might help me feel better is ...

_____

_____

_____

_____

_____

_____

Picture of me doing this ...

Someone who I would like to share my feelings with is _____.

I will do this by talking to them / writing them a note. (Circle one)

Dear _____,

Today I feel _____

because _____

_____

_____

_____

_____

_____

_____

_____

_____

_____

_____

_____

_____

_____

_____

*The back of this page is left blank so that you can draw a picture of how you feel and tear this page out of your journal to give someone your message.

Date: _____

Today I feel _____.

😊 😍 😜 😟 😢 😁 😠

This is a picture of how I'm feeling today ...

I feel this way because ...

_____
_____
_____
_____
_____
_____
_____

Something that might help me feel better is ...

_____

_____

_____

_____

_____

_____

Picture of me doing this ...

Someone who I would like to share my feelings with is _____.

I will do this by talking to them / writing them a note. (Circle one)

Dear _____,

Today I feel _____

because _____

_____

_____

_____

_____

_____

_____

_____

_____

_____

_____

_____

_____

_____

*The back of this page is left blank so that you can draw a picture of how you feel and tear this page out of your journal to give someone your message.

Date: _____

Today I feel _____.

😊 😍 😜 😟 😢 😬 😠

This is a picture of how I'm feeling today ...

I feel this way because ...

_____
_____
_____
_____
_____
_____
_____

Something that might help me feel better is ...

_____
_____
_____
_____
_____
_____

Picture of me doing this ...

Someone who I would like to share my feelings with is _____.

I will do this by talking to them / writing them a note. (Circle one)

Dear _____,

Today I feel _____

because _____

_____

_____

_____

_____

_____

_____

_____

_____

_____

_____

_____

_____

_____

*The back of this page is left blank so that you can draw a picture of how you feel and tear this page out of your journal to give someone your message.

Printed in Great Britain
by Amazon

The Big Time

A Memoir

by

Ingrid Lucia

The Big Time by Ingrid Lucia

ISBN: 978-1-62880-251-1

Copyright 2022 Ingrid Lucia. All rights reserved.

Except as permitted under U.S. Copyright Act of 1976, no part of book may be reproduced, distributed, or transmitted in any form or by any means, or stored in a database or retrieval system, without the prior written permission of the copyright owner.

This book was written between 2015 and 2022.

The names of some individuals have been changed to protect their identity.

Editors: Angie Joachim and Paula Underwood Winters

Cover Design/Layout: Paula Underwood Winters

Printed in the United States of America

For more info on Ingrid Lucia, including tour dates and music, email Ingrid.l.marshall@gmail.com

Published by:
Published by Westview